DSC SPEED READS

MANAGEMENT

Risk Management

Elizabeth Gray-King

directory of social change

Published by the Directory of Social Change (Registered Charity no. 800517 in England and Wales)

Head office: Resource for London, 352 Holloway Rd, London N7 6PA

Northern office: Suite 103, 1 Old Hall Street, Liverpool L3 9HG

Tel: 08450 77 77 07

Visit www.dsc.org.uk to find out more about our books, subscription funding websites and training events. You can also sign up for e-newsletters so that you're always the first to hear about what's new.

The publisher welcomes suggestions and comments that will help to inform and improve future versions of this and all of our titles. Please give us your feedback by emailing publications@dsc.org.uk

It should be understood that this publication is intended for guidance only and is not a substitute for professional advice. No responsibility for loss occasioned as a result of any person acting or refraining from acting can be accepted by the authors or publisher.

Print and digital editions first published 2009
Reprinted 2016

ISBN 978 1 906294 17 5

British Library Cataloguing in Publication Data
A catalogue record for this book is available from the British Library

Cover and text design by Kate Griffith
Typeset by Marlinzo Services, Frome
Print edition produced by Martins of Berwick

Contents

Introduction

Who will this book help?

This book is a risk management guide for employees or volunteers in smaller and community-based charities who find themselves unexpectedly in serious management. You may not be sure of professional business language and culture, yet have to understand it. You are all too aware of what could go wrong in your own organisation, but may not have learned the tools to assess and manage those possibilities.

Rather than high-level risk (such as trustee compliance or failure to create strategy), this book focuses on project risk at the grass roots – the small details which can make an organisation fail or succeed.

What will it give you?

This book aims to unpack risk. It will help you to understand that looking at what could go wrong and planning what you might do about it is far more about creativity and being prepared than it is about fulfilling some external requirement. It will give you the language and the tools to meet risk head on and to create appropriate responses to it. It includes a blank risk management plan on page 14 for you to refer to as you go along and use as a basis for your own plan.

Chapter 1

Defining risk

This chapter defines risk and risk management and demonstrates its usefulness.

Let's begin with a story.

Case study

A credit union in a socially deprived area had one employee – the manager. The trustee board thought it was unlikely that she would leave. But as it happened she unexpectedly put in her notice, so the job then had to be advertised.

But this wasn't all bad news... Some time ago, the supervisory committee (a sub-committee of the board of trustees) conducted a risk assessment and realised that, although it was unlikely that she would leave, the whole organisation was at risk if this single employee was not available for work. All the other staff were volunteers and didn't have the kind of operational knowledge she held. Also, it assessed that if marketing was not done in a planned way, there might not be enough customers to allow the credit union to achieve the financial stability that it wanted.

To reduce the risk, the committee took its assessment to the board. The board decided to appoint an assistant manager, in case of the manager's sudden departure, and to develop a marketing strategy.

Two people applied for the single post of assistant manager and both turned out to be terrific. Not wanting to lose talent, and having realised during its risk assessment that it was in the financial position to make two appointments, the credit union offered posts to both applicants. By doing the risk assessment, the committee and the board saved the credit union from a difficult situation. It meant that the board was prepared to make new appointments and that it could also grasp the opportunity of appointing an applicant who was strong on marketing. Despite the manager leaving, the board retained some continuity and had two strong internal candidates to apply for the vacant post.

Creative preparedness

This is a positive story on the back of what is often seen to be a dreary task – risk management. When it is a part of the day-to-day life of an organisation, good risk management is about being creatively prepared for anything. And that is what this book is about.

Case study

Elizabeth, a risk consultant who had worked with hundreds of organisations over many years, wished she could say that she'd seen more evidence of good practice. When visiting an organisation to help with its creative direction, she would ask the person responsible to see their risk management plan. More often than not, they would look blank and might recall that there was something about risk in an annual report somewhere … A few dusty heaps later, they would dig it out!

Other organisations would produce theirs rapidly, and in electronic format – an indicator that, wonderfully, the plans were used on a daily basis.

However, again and again she observed that these plans usually dealt with very high-level risk: preparing the board for its responsibilities or ensuring that managers are able to address legal requirements.

These high-level risk management plans weren't wrong: organisations should indeed have them in place. However, risk management needs to be far broader and more all-encompassing to support an organisation fully.

This book encourages you to look at risk management from a project manager's point of view rather than an accountant's: as a motivation to enliven projects, not just as being necessary by law.

Here is an example of risk management for a project with young people, and how it could be improved.

Case study

A youth organisation ran a project for young people under the age of 16. The board and organisers complied with the large number of laws that surrounds this age group. They drew up a simple risk management plan to address the legislation and made sure that all the right adults had the correct permissions and were doing what they should be. The risk management decision making sat at board level. The resulting practices then moved into the organisation where the right protocols were taught to those working directly with the young people.

This is correct risk management, but it is dry and functional. To manage risk creatively, however, you would suggest activities where the young people determine how their boundaries are managed. As an organiser, you would be there to support and supervise. You would provide a safe place where the adults facilitate the decisions that the young people make. They could create new projects themselves and apply for money for them. You and your colleagues would help the process and agree the boundaries, but the young people would drive the project. There is managed risk in this situation, but it is creative and inclusive.

Try to bring risk out of the usually negative and largely financial world in which it is often discussed: think of it as far more than simply managing what could go wrong. If you address risk early on in the life of your organisation or project, and look at what could go wrong in all areas – including and beyond finance – you can find the process to be a creative and exciting exercise.

By analysing what could go wrong, you can bring out ideas for ways to make sure that things go right – and from the outset, not in retrospect after a problem occurs. If you deal with risk up front you can ensure that the risk management is creative and becomes embedded in the life of an organisation or project.

Top tip

Address risk at the planning stage before any activity has been carried out, or even any funds identified. This can make a profound and positive difference to a project.

What is risk?

A common definition of risk is exposure to the chance of injury or loss. Put simply, risk is exposure to something that could go wrong – not being prepared for an adverse event. For example, if you go out in a downpour without a raincoat, you risk the adversity of getting wet.

Where next?

What is risk management? AskNCVO: www.ncvo-vol.org.uk/ask ncvo/index.asp ?id=2618& terms=risk

Another example is driving on a busy motorway without having checked your tyres regularly – you would risk a blow-out at the least, and a full motorway pile-up in the worst case scenario.

Risk is leaving yourself, your family, your organisation – anything – open to calamity.

The Charity Commission suggests that major risks are:

> *'those events which, if they occur, would have a severe impact on operational performance, objectives or reputation of the charity and which have a high likelihood of occurring.'*

We risk our organisations if we go into service delivery unplanned and unprotected. In the case study on page 5, the credit union could have risked its organisation's life by entrusting all the management to one employee, and risked its sustainability by not addressing marketing. If it had continued with that one employee and little marketing, there would have been a severe adverse impact on performance. It would not have been able to fulfil its objectives easily and, if left unaddressed, the risks would have continued.

A lack of marketing would have meant fewer new customers. This in turn would have meant little profit to distribute.

The organisation's reputation would have suffered, with customers realising that they were not served consistently and that they seldom received their share of any profit as dividends. A small amount of creative preparedness went a long way to avoid this calamity.

What is risk management?

We have established that good risk management is about creative preparedness, and the preceding examples will have gone some way to illustrate this.

To elaborate, however, risk management is about planning to get that raincoat out and regularly checking its protectiveness. It won't always work, depending on how hard it is raining and how well waterproofed your coat is, but you avoid the danger of being completely drenched. Risk management is about checking your tyres regularly and being prepared with a spare. This doesn't mean that you won't get a flat tyre, just that you minimise the impact of the accident.

It is about the credit union looking at what could go wrong, thinking up solutions and making appointments which themselves will be monitored. And it is about being on top of the highest level strategy at an operational level.

This is where you should translate the big dreams and visions into regular practical activity, and where monitoring risk should become part of your day-to-day life.

You can be creative and forward-thinking with your risk management by identifying risks and then deciding on processes to accept, minimise, transfer or reduce them, or create a plan B. This book will take you through step by step and show you how to do this.

Top tip

Remember that although an effective risk management system can provide reports for trustees and external audiences, its primary purpose is for organisational strength.

At worst, risk analysis is a one-off exercise to include in an annual report. At best, it is part and parcel of what it means to run any enterprise, whether charitable or otherwise, and it can be an endless source of inspiration.

The voluntary sector and risk management

Risk management has become increasingly important for the voluntary sector. The Charity Commission puts a legal requirement on larger, audited charities to say clearly whether the trustees have considered major risks and designed a system to manage them. Although smaller charities are not required to meet this regulation, it is often these charities that are most vulnerable to adverse events – their very size puts them at risk.

When should it be done?

Try to make imaginative and robust risk management part of your daily routine, like drinking tea or working through emails, or like wearing a raincoat without thinking about it. You should carry it out using clear systems and agreed information so that your organisation can:

- respond to risks with knowledge
- include risk management routines in day-to-day organisational activity
- be flexible enough to manage external and internal changes
- understand the risks well enough to take any failings to the right part of the organisation (leaders, managers, trustees, etc.).

Where next?

For further information about Charity Commission requirements, see: www.charity commission.gov.uk/ investigations/ charriskapp.asp

How to deal with risk

The first step is to nominate someone in the organisation – a lead – who will monitor the whole of the risk management plan. This could be a trustee, other volunteer or employee, depending on the size of the organisation. It is important that you have an *active* risk management lead: a risk plan needs to be in active operational use, not written for the sake of a report or a proposal. Even if your organisation is tiny, you will need a single individual to manage the risk plan. Seldom will the lead do the activities to manage the risks – they will appoint or ensure that there are individual risk leads even if, for example, it is explaining to a games leader volunteer how to manage the risks associated with those games.

The overall lead will ensure that the whole plan is monitored and updated regularly. This need not be an onerous task (unless your organisation is huge), but it does need to be part of regular project management.

Once you have a lead, they or a group gathered to think about risk should figure out what could go wrong and create a list. Then they should work through the list, sort the entries into categories according to the type of risk and establish who it would affect. For example, if the worst were to happen, would it be important internally, or could it have legal implications or a negative impact on other organisations or communities?

After the risks are sorted, the lead should analyse the likelihood of their occurrence, and if so, the possible severity of the consequences. Finally, they should make a plan for serious risks, planning well in advance what processes could be put in place and how to monitor whether they are happening.

Where next?

Risk Management, K Dickie, published by Volunteering England, 2003. A guide to the essentials of risk management for organisations that involve volunteers.

Chapter 2

Identifying risks

This chapter looks at the risk register – where you identify and draw up a list of risks.

The risk register

A risk register sounds like a formal, mysterious beast. At its simplest, it is a list of potential risks. You should begin your list by looking at each area of your organisation (or each task area of a project within the organisation) and asking questions such as:

- What could go wrong?
- What could go wrong with our planned timings?
- What could go wrong if X did not happen in the way we intend?
- What could go wrong if Y went completely askew?
- Could there be theft?
- Could there be vandalism?
- What would our standing in the community be if Z happened?
- What if we can't get our reports done in time?
- What if we lose our key leader?

Where next?

Managing Risk: Guidelines for medium-sized organisations, C Clark, NCVO, 2001. This was written to help management committee members and staff with undertaking a tailored risk analysis.

Listing risks

The best thing is simply to start – there is no absolutely right formula and no perfect format. See the sample plan on the following page as an example of what you can use. The risks should be listed under the 'Description' heading, with any more detail you may want in the 'Notes' column. The 'Description' is clear words about what could happen and the 'Notes' are why this is a risk.

For inspiration, you could look at a project or organisational plan. You may find a statement of planned activity in the middle of the funding application for a project. There might be an overall list of organisational objectives; or there may be an action plan, timetable or list of activities in the middle of a promotional brochure. For projects, you might find a task timetable (perhaps a Gantt chart or a list of outcomes and milestones).

Look at everything your organisation or project says that it will do and make a list of what could happen to hinder that intention. What could stop or weaken the activity? If you are working on your own, it is helpful to talk to others in your organisation's area of work or to borrow other risk lists for ideas.

Kinds of risk

It is helpful to compile your first list by thinking of what could go wrong under some different headings. Chapter 3 details the formal types, but the following groups will help you with your thinking.

People

Think about whether there is a risk of people not having sufficient training, not understanding their role or not being there. If your organisation relies on one

Where next?

For more information on Gantt Charts (graphical representations of the duration of tasks against the progression of time), see an example from The Open University: http://openlearn. open.ac.uk/mod/ resource/view.php ?id=261599

Top tip

When putting your list together, play the sceptic, the critical friend, the devil's advocate. Think of anything that could go wrong – this will become your risk register.

No.	Type	Date identified	Date of last update	Description	Notes	Priority	Action	Monitoring activity	Lead	Timing
1	F, O	12/12/2008	10/11/2009	Not enough participants	There aren't enough participants to make activities viable; risk of reduced finance and operational failure	H	▪ Create marketing strategy appropriate to target groups ▪ Train activity champions to market for more participants ▪ Modify marketing activity when trends demand	▪ Keep daily attendance figures ▪ Monitor weekly attendance trends ▪ Monitor monthly attendance trends	Activity leader	Review quarterly
2	O, C, E	12/12/2008	10/11/2009	Venue is unsafe	Equipment and environment not up to quality; risk of non-delivery of activity affecting operations, potential compliance risk and reputation	M	▪ Ensure daily checks of equipment ▪ Ensure equipment is regularly maintained ▪ Establish environmental safety checklist; use at each activity prep ▪ Create alternative venue register	▪ Monitor maintenance schedules monthly ▪ Check safety checklists	Centre manager	Review monthly

paid project manager and volunteers, as did the credit union, you would note the risk of that project manager suddenly being absent.

Equipment and other resources

Equipment and resource risks could be around access, upkeep, legislation or availability. What if your activity equipment suddenly fell apart? What if you had an amazing piece of kit, but there was no one properly trained to use it?

Finance

Finance risks not only include the scenario where someone could run off with the cash box; there are also risks around spending too much on key resources or relying on fundraising for a core service. What if a donated piece of equipment is too expensive to maintain? Of course an organisation is at risk if its funding runs out, and this is a usual risk to name. However, it could be that the funding is not renewed because the organisation has not managed its projects robustly enough. There might be much smaller risks at operational level which mean that a funder could lose confidence in the organisation.

Legislation

Risks around legislation include having to comply with laws and duties and conducting Criminal Records Bureau checks for workers with children and vulnerable adults. There is also legislation around insurance, health and safety and more.

If you are unsure about what laws affect your organisation, do take guidance. You can go to your local Citizens Advice Bureau for some guidance, and they may be able to advise you on where to get a pro bono lawyer if you need one.

Top tip

Make sure you have appropriate signs around your building, including health and safety, fire and first aid.

Shireen Mustafa, Head of Customer Services and Facilities, DSC

Where next?

Common legal pitfalls for charities, see: www.russell-cooke.co.uk/news_articles_legalpitfalls.htm

Chapter 3

Sorting risk into types

Not all risks are the same kind or at the same level of importance. This chapter discusses how to categorise and prioritise your list.

Risk management begins with sorting your list into manageable slices.

First, you should separate the risks into types. This will help you a great deal in managing them, as not all parts of your organisation will need to deal with all of the risks. Furthermore, it will make a long list into a number of shorter ones, and for that reason will be more controllable.

Second, you can delegate the next stages – analysis and creative preparedness – to a number of individuals or groups.

What are the risk types?

Even a small search of risk management guidance reveals that risks are separated into a range of types: it depends on who is writing the guidance and for whom. There are lists with as few as three types (governance, operations and finance), six types (strategic, operational, financial, people, regulatory and governance) and dozens of types in a number of operational areas.

Most of the readers of this book will be working in the voluntary and community sector, so the Charity Commission's guidelines seem to be the most appropriate. However, you should note that the Commission risk types are listed within the guidance on audit and financial reporting in *Charity Statement of Recommended Practice, Accounting and Reporting (revised 2005)*.

This book (SORP 2005) advocates that you perform risk management across the whole of your organisation. With this in mind, the examples given here under the Charity Commission's categories apply to all of an organisation's activities, not just finance.

The SORP 2005 breaks down risk categories into five types.

1 **Governance risks** – such as inappropriate organisational structure, difficulties recruiting trustees with relevant skills, conflict of interest.
2 **Operational risks** – such as service quality and development, contract pricing, employment issues, health and safety issues, fraud and misappropriation.
3 **Financial risks** – such as accuracy and timeliness of financial information, adequacy of reserves and cash flow, diversity of income sources, investment management.
4 **External risks** – such as public perception and adverse publicity, demographic changes, government policy.
5 **Compliance risks: law and regulation** – such as breach of trust law, employment law and regulatory requirements around particular activities such as fundraising or running care facilities.

To understand the types, it may be helpful to think of them as 'internal' (1 to 3) and 'external' risks (4 and 5).

Where next?

Charity Statement of Recommended Practice, Accounting and Reporting (revised 2005) available from: www.charity-commission.gov.uk/Library/publications/pdfs/sorp05text colour.pdf

Top tip

Ensure that your employees are adequately trained to perform all of their duties, such as manual handling training for those doing physical work.

Shireen Mustafa, Head of Customer Services and Facilities, DSC

Internal risks

The checklists under each heading cover some of the major areas that you should examine (but they are not comprehensive). You can use them as a starting point by ticking off the issues you have addressed. In this way you can identify some areas that need attention.

Governance risks

This type includes all kinds of risks about management structure and arrangements for effective internal governance. In this category, consider your internal organisational structures and their ability to support or hinder the purpose of the organisation.

Checklist

❑ Are the right people doing the right jobs at the right level?

❑ Does your chair of trustees relate well to the operational manager? If not, there could be a risk of key messages from trustees never making it to the organisation, or of key needs for decisions never being brought to trustees' meetings.

❑ Could any of your trustees personally benefit from the organisation's activities? If so, there should be a list of any conflicts of interest to show that the organisation is aware of them.

Operational risks

This type used to be called 'project risks'. It is helpful to think of items under this heading as related to the internal operations behind the activities of your organisation or project.

Checklist

❑ If your organisation charges fees or sells goods, are the prices right? If too high, operations could fail as the market won't purchase; if too low, operations could be underfunded.

❑ How is your service quality?

❑ How clean is any venue that you use? Is the maintenance of the venues up to scratch? Might there be health and safety risks if not?

❑ How effective is your publicity? Does it reflect the mission and purpose of your organisation in the best light? If not, there is a risk of the organisation or project not attracting or keeping its target clients or beneficiaries.

❑ Are your employment arrangements correct? Does everyone have a contract, terms and conditions and a job description? Without these arrangements, key employees will be able to leave without warning, which will put the physical operation at risk.

❑ Do your organisation's employees understand their job roles, and can the organisation rely on them? If not, the physical operation is left unprotected in the case of operational failure.

❑ What about fraud and misappropriation? Do you have measures in place to monitor money and resources?

The point on fraud and misappropriation might seem to be a financial risk, but it is actually about operational procedures being robust enough to prevent theft or misuse of resources. If you have no clear procedures in place and someone is able to run away with resources, the organisation is at risk of being unable to operate.

Financial risks

This is often the easiest risk type to understand. Of course, it is about accuracy and timeliness of financial information, but it is also about having the right levels of money in savings or held for dedicated projects.

In addition, financial risks are about cash flow and diversity of income sources. For larger social benefit organisations, investment management could be a

Where next?

DSC runs courses on health and safety and risk assessment. Go to www.dsc.org.uk/ Training/ Humanresources for more details.

Top tip

If you rely on one supplier, say for sports equipment or website support, what would happen if they went out of business overnight? Are alternatives available, how soon and at what price?

John Hoare, Business Consultant

financial risk. In an increasing climate of transparent ethical investment, a charitable organisation could be at risk if its own investment does not reflect the ethics of its mission and purpose.

Checklist

❑ Do you have measures in place to protect funds raised for a specific part of the organisation or for a particular project? If not, your organisation is at risk if it diverts money, and might not be able to return it if the designated project does not start.

❑ Do you have an effective system to watch the ups and downs of income and expenditure?

❑ Is your organisation dependent on a few key income streams, and would it be at risk if one of them dried up?

External risks

Risks of this type relate to what could put your organisation at risk in terms of its reputation or its geographic or target group commitment.

Reputation and demographics

Checklist

❑ What would happen to public perception of your organisation, and its reputation, if an accident or negative event were to occur? Do you have strategies in place to deal with this?

❑ What impact would demographic changes have on your organisation?

For example, if someone was injured in an activity project and you had not planned ahead for such an instance, it could result in a serious image problem, fuelled by adverse publicity. The public perception of the organisation's ability would be less positive than before the incident. This is a risk about external reputation.

Moreover, some demographic changes could have a negative impact on your organisation's ability to work in its physical location or with its target group. If your organisation is set up to give support to an elderly care home that closes, the organisation is then at risk.

Compliance risks

This type covers everything around the law and compliance with it.

Checklist

- ☐ Is your organisation always able to comply with, for example, employment law? This might mean always having enough reserve funds to pay for an employee's redundancy.
- ☐ If your organisation keeps information on its beneficiaries, are you clear on what information can be shared and what permissions you need? (If not, you are at risk of breaking trust law and of not complying with data protection legislation.)
- ☐ Do your premises comply with health and safety legislation?
- ☐ What about volunteers and staff? Is it obvious that equal opportunity legislation has been followed in their recruitment and appointment?

Although compliance risks are largely about complying with external and often imposed legislation, they also can relate to compliance with an organisation's objectives. For example, if a community theatre operating in Ely decided to work with a similar rural community in Buxton, this puts the organisation at risk, as it would be working beyond its geographical objectives. There is the risk that its insurance would become invalid in case of any accidents or that, if the organisation is a charity, it would be acting outside the remit of its constitution.

Case study

A long-established organisation was originally set up to fulfil a specific remit within a community, but 50 years on the community had changed. This became a risk to the organisation's continuing ability to meet its objectives. Set up during 'flavour of the month' funding, the organisation found that government priorities had changed, and so it had to change its purpose to avoid risking closure.

Top tip

Security isn't just about technical measures – locks and passwords. These are no good if people forget to turn the key, or if they give their password to someone else. Human behaviour is often your biggest source of risk.

Paul Ticher, Consultant. Author of Data Protection, DSC, 2009

Multiple risks

Risks can fall under more than one heading. For example, failing to submit accounts on time would be both a finance and a compliance risk. This also could be a governance risk, which would make the failure to submit accounts a three-heading risk.

A risk of accident on an outing could be operational and external. If an accident happened, it could mean people don't attend future outings and it could give the organisation a bad reputation. It would be rare for one risk to be categorised as all types, but not impossible.

If you use the risk management sample plan in this book, the 'Notes' section is where you explain how one risk could fall under multiple headings.

Spreading the work

Once all the risks are sorted into types, distribute the risk list for analysis (see chapter 4) and mitigation planning (see chapter 5). It is very rare for one person or even one group of people to know how to manage all the risks in all the categories.

You could give compliance risks to trustees or to an external legal team that regularly works with your charity. The governance risk list could be given to some strategy experts and the external risk list to those who understand both the community around the organisation and government policy.

You could give the financial risk list to those who understand financial management and resource use, and the operational risk list to those who know how the organisation is run on a day-to-day basis.

Sorting risk into types makes the job easier. It spreads the work around an organisation, increasing the chance that managing risk will become a ordinary daily activity. In the sample plan these types are noted with their first letter (G, O, F, E, C) in the second column.

Chapter 4

Analysing risk

You now have a list of risks categorised. This chapter looks at the next stage: assessing the likelihood of each potential incident and, if any come to pass, understanding the possible impact on the organisation.

Assessment

To decide how important the risks are and what action you may need to take, analyse the risks to determine how likely they are and what impact they could have. After sorting into types, this is the next way to reduce a huge list of risks into a manageable risk plan.

It would be a waste of time and energy – not to say deeply frustrating – to develop full risk management plans for each risk, whatever its priority. However, high-priority risks must have a clear plan to mitigate them. This is because their impact is so significant that, if they occur, they could truly damage an organisation.

There is no magic or mystery to analysing risks. With time and experience a risk analysis can be a relatively speedy exercise. However, it is worth devoting time and energy to the first few times you do it.

Likelihood

The first step is to figure out how likely it would be for identified risks to occur. Look at each risk in turn and ask: 'How likely is this to happen?' and 'Would it really

> **Top tip**
>
> **Use risk analysis to identify those risks for which you should take time and effort to create a risk management plan, and for which you should do mild, incremental monitoring.**

ever occur?' Judging the likelihood of a risk is simply a matter of applying a little creative common sense.

For example, in the case of a coach outing, it would be unlikely (although not impossible) for the coach to crash. So, 'coach crashes' would be an entry on your community centre outing risk register, and it would be judged unlikely.

However, think of a busy community club as members come in and pay their subscriptions. It is highly likely that the volunteers who are receiving the subscription money may not know the members, or might not remember to allocate the subscription as they receive the money. So, 'not applying subs to members' would be an entry in the community centre outing risk register, and marked as highly likely. For the credit union case study on page 5, having no clear marketing management was highly likely, yet the possibility of the manager leaving was unlikely.

Continue the process by working through each risk listed in the register and assessing its likelihood along a spectrum of six measures:

1   extremely unlikely
2   unlikely
3   moderately likely
4   regular occurrence
5   highly likely
6   extremely likely – frequent occurrence.

Impact

After the likelihood question, you can reduce the risk list further by asking the following questions.

■   What impact would this have on our organisation?
■   If it happened, how bad would it be?

You may identify a risk as extremely unlikely, but if it did happen, it could have a hugely negative impact. In the case of a potential coach crash, the impact would be enormous, bringing real grief and loss to the organisation. It could be fundamental to continuing operations, and perhaps even threaten the organisation's existence.

However, a risk can be very likely but have almost no impact. In the case of subscription monies not being attributed to the right club member, the impact is not critical, just a case of following up some discrepancies. It would have a significant impact in the long term only if it were a regularly occurring risk which was not managed. For the credit union case study, poor marketing would have a significant impact in the medium term while, although the manager's departure would be unlikely, this event would be fundamental to continuing operations.

Impact measures

Continue your risk analysis by looking at each risk already judged by likelihood and assessing the impact along a spectrum of six measures:

1 not critical
2 minor impact in some areas
3 minor impact in many areas
4 significant impact – would not affect continued operations in the short term, but might in the long term
5 significant impact in the medium term – relates to substantial operational areas
6 fundamental to continuing operations.

You can assess your whole risk list by how likely the risks are first, and then judge the levels of impact second. Alternatively you could assess the list by taking each risk one at a time, judging its likelihood and assessing its impact before moving on to the next risk.

Priority

The last stage of risk analysis is to combine the results of the likelihood and impact assessments in order to

Where next?

Go to www.kingston smith.co.uk/ Kingston-Smith/ Sectors/ Charities.htm and click (under 'Links') on the website's link to its online publication: *Risk Management Guide.*

prioritise risks as low, medium or high. You can do this by multiplying the result of the likelihood analysis by the result of the impact analysis, using the numbers attached to measures, as shown below. A final score of 1 to 9 = low priority, 10 to 19 = medium priority and 20 or over = high priority.

For example, the risk 'coach crash' was analysed as unlikely (2), but fundamental to continuing operations (6), giving a score of 12 (2 x 6), placing the risk in the medium priority area. 'Not applying subs to members' was analysed as highly likely (5), but not critical (1), giving a score of 5 (5 x 1), making it as a low-priority risk.

The following matrix is often used alongside a risk register. It helps you to work methodically through each individual risk.

Impact / Likelihood	1 Extremely unlikely	2 Unlikely	3 Moderately likely	4 Likely	5 Highly likely	6 Extremely likely
1 Not critical	1	2	3	4	5	6
2 Minor impact in some areas	2	4	6	8	10	12
3 Minor impact in many areas	3	6	9	12	15	18
4 Significant impact; would not affect continued operations in the short term but might in the long term	4	8	12	16	20	24
5 Significant impact in medium term, relates to substantial operational areas	5	10	15	20	25	30
6 Fundamental to continuing operations	6	12	18	24	30	36

Priority

Low	1 to 9
Medium	10 to 19
High	Over 20

Once you have analysed all the risks, you can mark each risk as low, medium or high priority. In the sample plan on page 14 you can enter your agreed priorities under the 'Priority' heading. Add any more detail you want to in the 'Notes' column.

You should apply your common sense when using this matrix. Check whether every risk that you believe should have a high impact has come out at that level in the matrix. You might want to move something from low to medium or high (or vice versa) if your experience and knowledge suggests that this is appropriate.

For example, your risk analysis shows the potential risk that your charity's chief executive suddenly disappears. This is extremely unlikely (score 1), but it would be fundamental to continuing operations (score 6). At a total of 6, it would be a low risk. However, common sense dictates that a risk management plan would need to be drawn up in the case of any key employee suddenly being unavailable for any reason.

The analysed risk register is important for a huge range of reasons, not least of which is that it reduces a nightmare risk list to a manageable one. If your organisation is short on time, this is a great benefit. A more important reason is that it proves that your organisation has spotted and considered potential weaknesses.

Chapter 5

Mitigating and managing risk

After listing, sorting into types and analysis, the real risk management begins. This chapter explains how to take your prioritised risks into the area of risk management.

You now need to make some plans to manage all the risks which have come out as medium or high in your analysis. This is where the fun begins: the creative, inspirational work referred to in chapter 1.

Risk management plans include mitigation measures and monitoring activity.

Mitigation measures

Start managing the risks by looking at each one and creating a set of mitigation actions. These actions should make each risk less severe, less likely or have a smaller impact. The actions will include any of a number of measures to:

- accept the risk
- minimise the impact of risk
- transfer the risk
- reduce the likelihood of risk
- deploy fallback plans – create a plan B.

In the sample plan on page 14, the mitigation measures you come up with should be listed under the 'Actions' heading. Any more detail can be added to the 'Notes' section. If you complete the plan in this way, it can form the core of your risk management. Day-to-day risk management will involve monitoring the plan at agreed intervals to make sure that the risk activity leads (see page 11) feed back their monitoring information at arranged times. You should also make sure that the leads fully understand the information and implications of the risks that they directly manage.

Accept the risk

You won't need to do much to accept a risk, and there won't be much monitoring activity. The point about naming an acceptable risk and keeping it in your plan is to demonstrate that your organisation understands there are risks that it will knowingly bear, and knows what action it could take, if necessary.

Minimise the impact of risk

Every day we do things to try to minimise the impact of risk. In case of an accident, you might wear protective gear to minimise the danger of head injury when cycling. If you organised a climbing activity day, you and your fellow climbers would wear helmets in case of a fall. And you might take spare cash should the activity leader have cash stolen.

You set out knowing the potential risks and wear or do something that could minimise the impact if anything bad were to happen.

A children's playground will have rubber or mulched space under a climbing frame to minimise the impact of a fall. This is almost an acceptance of risk, as mentioned previously, but involves much more active measures to mitigate the risk.

Case study

An activity centre located on a rockface accepted that there was a risk of rock falls. This was on the understanding that people who engage in adventure activities can expect a degree of risk in the environment. The centre's risk management action was to put measures in place to ensure that if a rock fall did occur they would be able to deal with it. For example, they prominently displayed the up-to-date mountain rescue phone number on a poster in the centre. This was low-level risk management, but demonstrated clear awareness.

Top tip

Insure your risks: if you're selling goods or services check that you have adequate insurance to cover all of these activities.

**Shireen Mustafa,
Head of Customer
Services and
Facilities, DSC**

Case study

An interactive garden for people with disabilities had a befriending system where experienced garden users accompanied new users. This system included training and support for the experienced garden users in order to reduce the likelihood of potential injuries.

Transfer the risk

Transferring a risk is a simple way to manage the big things. It is insurance for the wildly unlikely or the very costly. It is delegation to experts who understand. The activity centre in the case study understands activities, but it has insurance for the minibus in case of damage, and probably breakdown cover in case the minibus suddenly stops. The staff understand how to use particular equipment, but they delegate to experts for its regular service and have it insured against breakdown, damage or theft. Although transferring the risk could encourage the organisation to say 'It wasn't my fault, I delegated it', the final responsibility remains with this organisation, the contractor. Transferring the risk of an event to an events management firm does not protect the organisation from the negative impact, should the event fail.

Reduce the likelihood of risk

This is the type of risk mitigation where you can really use creative preparedness. How can you stop a risk happening at all or reduce the incidence of it? You can give training, maintain resources, share information and regularly monitor the state of processes or resources. By training people you will help them to understand how to prevent risk in the first place. By sharing information you can introduce or reinforce facts that people should know in order to reduce risk. For example, hospitals use posters to explain how germs are transferred and the 'Now wash your hands' signs to show how to prevent the spread of germs.

You put mitigation measure in place to help people understand that changing, or being aware of, their own behaviours can reduce risk for many people.

Deploy fallback plans

This is about having a plan B. You mitigate risk by having a fallback plan. You create an alternative activity in case the risk occurs, so that its impact on the organisation will not be as bad as it might have been.

However, you should consider all other options (accepting, minimizing, transferring, reducing likelihood) before creating a plan B. It can be far more work and use more resources to create an alternative scenario than to tweak an existing one to mitigate potential risk.

Monitoring activity

You have almost finished your plan. You have identified all potential risks and checked them with other people. You have shortened a horrendously long risk list, first by breaking it up into risk types, then by analysing it to allow low-priority risks to drop down to the bottom. You have given attention to the medium and high risks, and now have a range of mitigation measures, depending on the type of risk.

At this point it is time to go to the list with its measures and decide how you should collect information about the risk being managed, and how frequently you will want to monitor that information. Some measures will need to be monitored only infrequently.

For example, in the activity centre case study on page 29, if you have accepted the risk that rocks may fall, and your mitigation measure is to have up-to-date contact details of mountain rescue, usually this would not have to be monitored often. Perhaps once a year, to make sure the details are correct. However, if you have equipment in heavy use where the risk of injury is great, you would want to:

- check the equipment on an activity-by-activity basis
- keep a record of all the checks
- schedule regular maintenance and reporting
- hear back at meetings where the management of equipment is an agenda item.

Case study

On an activity centre's expedition, canoes fell off the top of the minibus on the way to the lake and were damaged. This was not good but some alternative canoes had already been identified in a neighbouring activity centre and were able to be brought over quickly. The team had identified this as a potential risk and had created a plan B in case anything were to happen to the rack that the canoes were attached to.

In the sample plan on page 14, the monitoring activity is listed under the 'Monitoring activity' heading. You can add any more detail to the 'Notes' section.

Finally, as covered in chapter 1, it is important to have a lead person to manage each individual risk. This person should be closest to the potential risk and most aware of the risk management activity.

In the sample plan, that person will be named in the 'Lead' column. Under 'Timing' you should enter how often, as overall risk manager, you would expect to check the individual risk, or to receive reports about that risk.

The role of the overall risk manager, the operational risk lead, is to check that all measures are in place and to raise concerns where it is appropriate.

A word of warning: if you are both the project lead and the project deliverer – that is, if you are the only one who works in, and is responsible for, a project or an organisation – then it is essential to have this risk plan agreed by those who bear the final legal responsibility. While this situation itself (from a risk point of view) is not advisable, if you are the only one in charge, then your trustees or management group need to understand the full extent of risk and bear it with you.

The most important point made in this book has been that risk management is about creative preparedness. You will manage risk well if you link creative preparedness intimately to your project planning. Thorough risk analysis at the start of the project will create tasks (mitigation measures) which you can then add to the overall project plan. You should make active and ongoing risk management a part of any project planning process. By doing this, slowly but surely, you can change risk management from being a dry, dusty and painful requirement to something that is creative and inspirational.